Sumatran Tigers

By Alison Tibbitts and
Alan Roocroft

PUBLISHED BY

Capstone Press

Mankato, Minnesota USA

CIP
LIBRARY OF CONGRESS CATALOGING IN PUBLICATION DATA

Tibbitts, Alison.
  Sumatran tigers / by Alison Tibbitts and Alan Roocroft.
      p. cm. -- (Animals, animals, animals)
  Summary: Discusses the physical characteristics, behavior, and life cycle of Sumatran tigers and their current status as an endangered species.

  ISBN 1-56065-105-9
  1. Tigers--Indonesia--Sumatra--Juvenile literature. [1. Tigers--Indonesia--Sumatra. 2. Rare animals. 3. Wildlife conservation.]
  I. Roocroft, Alan. II. Title. III. Series: Tibbitts, Alison.
  Animals, animals, animals.
  QL737.C23T4743   1992
  599.74'428--dc20   92-11448
                                                      CIP
                                                      AC

Consultant:
John Turner, Lead Keeper
Tiger River Run
Zoological Society of San Diego

Photo Credits:
Alison Tibbitts and Alan Roocroft

Capstone Press
P.O. Box 669, Mankato, MN, U.S.A. 56002-0669

The afternoon is hot and humid in the jungle. A female Sumatran tiger cools herself in a secluded pond. She suffers in the heat, as do all tigers. She lies with her hindquarters in the water. Her front paws rest on the sandy bank. She waits for dusk when she will hunt for food again.

These cats are fast and quick. They **prey** on animals much larger and stronger than they are. After the hunt, they drag their kill to cover near a water hole. They guard it until all the food is gone. Only a few bones remain when the tiger has finished. Several days pass before the animal needs to hunt again.

Good tiger **habitats** are found in forests and wooded hillsides. Tigers also like to live in rainforests and mangrove swamps. The cats need only a few simple things for survival. They must have water, enough cover for protection, and prey. Tigers do not like to climb trees. They will if there is no other choice. They are excellent swimmers and sometimes swim in the open ocean. All of them like to play in the water.

Tigers on the island of Sumatra, in southeastern Asia, are small compared to others. Their fur is a soft orange-red color. The soft **undercoat** is a creamy shade. The head, body, tail, and **flanks** have heavy black stripes spaced close together. The striping pattern is a bit different for each tiger. Every cat has large white spots behind both ears. These spots help tigers find each other in tall grass. The spots guide cubs as they walk behind their mother.

Sumatran tigers' heads look square. They do not have the nose notch found in all other tigers. This makes their noses and foreheads meet in straight lines instead of a slope. Their heads look even more boxy because of their long cheek whiskers. There are no manes on their necks.

Tigers are usually alone, but they are not unsocial. They know about each other. When two or more are together, it is a courting pair or a mother with cubs. Tigers talk to each other with growls, roars, purrs, moans, grunts, whines, snarls, and snorts. They make a "chuffle" sound by blowing through their lips and noses. This is a friendly way to greet each other. Another sound Sumatran tigers make imitates the **"pok"** sound of their favorite prey, the **sambar** deer. This trick keeps the deer from realizing a tiger is near.

All cats mark their home range territory in the same ways. They spray urine and scrape the ground. Other cats see these signs and know the tigers are around. If a home range is not marked for a few weeks, another tiger takes it for himself.

The size of a home range depends on the kind of habitat and what prey lives there. The cats do not go into a range claimed by another tiger of the same sex. A male's range overlaps those of several females. The most important thing to him is to have females nearby. What he wants most is to father many cubs. Visiting tigers do not stay long in his territory.

Hunting takes up most of a tiger's time. It works alone, beginning at sundown. It depends on no one but itself for food. It may wait in ambush, but it would rather keep moving. Water holes are a good place to begin. Its hearing guides it as it **prowls** around. It depends on its yellow eyes only when it is close to its prey. Other animals often cry out or squeak to signal its presence.

The tiger crouches down when it spots what it wants. It holds its head steady as it moves slowly and carefully. It keeps its claws inside its paws. It touches the ground lightly with each foot before taking a step. It makes no noises that would warn the prey of danger. The tiger needs surprise on its side. It wants to attack with only a few leaps. Distance is important because it can run fast, but not for long.

When everything is right, the tiger rushes toward its prey from behind or from the side. Its weight knocks it off balance even if the prey is bigger than the tiger. The cat goes for the throat or the side of the neck. The prey cannot fight back.

A tiger uses his back legs for jumping. His front legs have heavy muscles for pulling and holding. His long claws clutch things tightly. He uses his forepaws the way humans use hands. Short fangs in his lower jaw hook onto prey. Long fangs in the upper jaw hold and shred it. A tiger needs all his tools. His hunt fails nine times out of ten, and he goes away hungry.

There are many stories about man-eating tigers. When a tiger kills a human, it is usually an accident. These animals defend themselves against what they see as a threat. A female protects her cubs with her life. Tigers rarely attack humans just for something to do.

The cats breed around the age of four. Two or three cubs are born in a cave or a hollow tree. The mother raises her babies alone. She devotes herself to nursing, cleaning, and guarding them. She hunts more often during the six months she nurses the cubs. She has to make enough milk for them.

Cubs are helpless at birth. They begin to follow their mother at two months. She shows them their first kill about this time. Cubs make their own kill before they reach one year old. They become independent soon after the age of two.

Sumatra's tiger country has many problems. Humans are moving in and changing forests into pastures and farmland. They shoot or poison tigers who attack their livestock. **Poaching** happens because tiger skins can be sold for a lot of money. The animals cannot reach each other to breed because their safe areas are not connected. There are fewer tigers for all these reasons.

There are only two hundred Sumatran tigers left in the world. Fifty of these are in breeding programs in zoos. It may be possible someday to return zoo tigers to the jungle after they are grown. Until that can happen, the Sumatran government is working on the wildlife problem. There is no time to waste. These rare and elegant cats have to depend on people. They cannot help themselves.

GLOSSARY / INDEX

Flank: the side of an animal between the ribs and hips (page 10)

Habitat: a special place to live for a long time (page 9)

Poaching: breaking the law by killing animals and selling their body parts (page 26)

Pok: a sound made by Sambar deer (page 14)

Prey: animals hunted and killed by another animal for food (page 6)

Prowl: wander about in search of prey (page 18)

Sambar: small Asian deer (page14)

Undercoat: soft layer of thick, short fur growing between the outer hair and the skin (page 10)